My Bangor Years:
A Reminiscence

by Lois Griffin Barnes

To Rob - You are blessed with a great spirit and zest for life. It is a gift - use it wisely! I love every bit of your enthusiasm - may it always be with you. I enjoy you immensely! and love you more than that! Remember me!

B'Lo

Westview Publishing Co., Inc.
Nashville, Tennessee

First Edition January 2005

Printed in the United States of America

ISBN 0-9764940-0-0

Layout and other pre-press work by
Westview Publishing Co., Inc.

Manuscript preparation by Susan B. Barnes

Westview Publishing Co., Inc.
8120 Sawyer Brown Road, Suite 107
Nashville, TN 37221
www.westviewpublishing.com

This book is dedicated to those family and friends who traveled along the "growing up" road with me in Bangor and Natarswi. The years hold warm memories and so I thank them all.

Lois Griffin Barnes
Nashville, Tennessee
2005

Mountains

God gave me mountains
With hills at their knees
Mountains too high
For the flutter of trees

Mountains that know
The dark valley of death
That have kissed a pale star
And felt its last breath

And still lift the dawn
On a golden rimmed cup
God gave me mountains
And the strength to climb up

Author unknown

Contents

Chapter One:

The Farm

The three-story white farmhouse stood on the southwest corner of Union Street (once called the avenue) and Griffin Road. It had, at a right angle, a long white shed, and connected to it, a big red barn. The year was 1931. Ella Frances Dudley Griffin had lived here alone since her husband, Fred, died in 1921. Ella kept good care of the premises, inside and out. She spring-cleaned with gusto. When the snow melted she dragged rugs outside for a beating, aired quilts, and scrubbed and polished. The shed was swept out, cobwebs banished. She kept no animals, not even a dog or a cat.

The farm itself consisted of 45 acres of pasture, orchard and trees. It had been part of a much larger tract of land that Thomas Jefferson Griffin, Fred's father, had accumulated beginning in 1850. Thomas's home had been a square, two-story white brick, on the northeast corner of Union Street and Griffin Road.

The lengthy obituary of Thomas Griffin notes that he was one of Bangor's oldest and most respected citizens when he died at the age of 92, in 1898.

In the spring of 1854 he had built a barn, and then the house with bricks that had been brought up Kenduskeag Stream in the winter on sleds and across the fields. He was described as a gentleman of high ideals, temperate, a Republican, and, in 1898, the oldest member of Hammond Street Congregational Church.

As a young man, Thomas and his brother Stephen hauled part of the brick and stone used in the building of the Bangor Theological Seminary. He had worked with one Nathaniel Hatch in setting out some of the large trees on Court and Ohio Streets. They were the beautiful elms which graced those streets for so many years.

Thomas married Asenath Wiley. They lived in the white brick on Union Street, and had seven children, one of whom lived only three years. Five sons and one daughter survived. One unmarried son, Heman, taught school and lived in the home place all his life.

The youngest son, Frederick Thomas, is the one to whom Ella was wed when she was a 16-year-old strawberry blonde. Fred was 34. She had grown up on the other side of Kenduskeag Stream on her father's dairy farm.

Albion Dudley, in 1835, settled in the area known then as the Sherburne District. Ella was one of four children, 2 boys and 2 girls. She was educated at Maine Central Institute in Pittsfield. Her old autograph book testifies to her popularity and wide circle of friends.

Fred and Ella had 26 years together. Their 15th anniversary was celebrated with a party in their home, March 12, 1900. I have a silver covered butter dish with the dates engraved, which their friends gave them. My father remembered the occasion well, as a big snowstorm came up. All the horses had to be put in the barn and the guests spent the night!

My father, Dudley, was their only child. He never really cared for the farm, but was much happier when he was in town. He was not accepted into the service for World War I because of a broken ankle that had not been properly set. Remington Arms, the gun maker, had a plant in Bridgeport, Connecticut. Dudley went there and worked until after 1918 when the war ended on the eleventh day of the eleventh month.

He returned to Bangor and on Valentine's Day in 1923, Dudley and Louise Elinor Nickerson were married by the Rev. Arthur M. Little of Hammond Street Congregational Church in a small home ceremony. Louise had graduated from Bangor High in 1918 and the Eastern Maine General Hospital training school in the class of 1921. They were a popular couple with a wide circle of friends. Louise was vivacious and one who like to organize outings and good times.

Chapter Two:

Myself

Louise and Dudley had three daughters. Elinor was born in December of 1923, Grace in July of 1926, and Lois in 1931. I am that Lois. I have no recollection of my mother, because she became very ill in the winter of 1934. I was sent to the farm to stay with Grammie Griffin, and as my mother did not recover but died shortly, I stayed on the farm. They were happy years and I have many fond memories of them. My grandmother Griffin was gentle, but strong, and took on the management of a two-year-old with great aplomb. It seemed to give her a new zest for living.

As in many a household, life seemed to center in the kitchen, especially during the long, cold Maine winters. The center of the kitchen was a big, polished, black, wood-burning stove. It had a tank on one end, which, when filled with water, provided hot water for us all winter. There was also the ever present tea-kettle. A built-in wood box was kept filled by carrying armloads of wood from the shed. Dudley converted this stove to an oil-burning unit, and from then on that chore was obsolete! My cat, which came with me, would lie on the old wood box by the stove. When

The old farm house

Lois - 6th grade

Lois, D.G., and Grace Griffin

Elinor and Grace Griffin

it came time for a hot bath, the tub would be brought in and placed on a big braided rug in front of the stove, hot water poured in, and voila!

By a window in the kitchen was Grandmother's wicker rocking chair and by it was my play area, a small red table and chairs, and a chest with my toys. One drawer in the chest had some of her things in it, including a flat stick, about like a ruler, with which she used to threaten a recalcitrant child! It was rarely ever used, but I did know it would sting the backs of my legs, so guess I was not always so well-behaved that punishment was completely foreign!

A dining room, off the kitchen, had a walk-in china closet. Shelves surrounded the wall, and beautiful china sat on the shelves. Blue Chelsea Grape pieces, bowls, cups and saucers, goblets and glassware. A pair of salt and pepper shakers was a favorite of mine, and I was allowed to play with them on the dining table. One shaker was a boy, with a black hat and long brown coat. The other, a girl in bonnet, coat, and muff.

The bedroom was downstairs where Grammie and I slept. She had a white iron bed and I had a single bed with a feather mattress. We warmed our sheets in winter with a soapstone that had been heated in the oven, wrapped in paper and a flannel cover, and then put in the foot of the bed to keep our toes warm.

In winter when the aurora borealis, northern lights, were colorful and beautiful, Grammie would get me up to stand at the window to admire the beauty.

One winter night a neighbor across the way lost his barn to a fire, spontaneous combustion in the hay they said.

The spectacle was awesome as the colors lit up the night and reflected on the snow.

The long Maine winters were a time for a fertile imagination to be developed in a child who had no playmates. On Saturday mornings I sat on the floor in front of the radio and listened to a program called "Let's Pretend". I loved listening to the stories, and my mind developed its own pictures.

Grandmother read to me a great deal; the Bobbsey Twins and Honey Bunch series were a few of my favorites. My father would come to the house with my sisters, and pull out from the shelf a worn and much-loved book of Longfellow poems. He would read, with expression, the tales of Hiawatha, Evangeline, and "The Midnight Ride of Paul Revere"! We needed no print for the last one; we all learned it by heart. I recited it to my children on Patriot's Day and they carry on the tradition!

We could walk across the field by the long snow fences in winter and come to a frozen brook. It was small, but Grace, Elinor, and I would find a few patches of ice large enough to skate on. The snowdrifts in front of the fences provided wonderful opportunities for snow forts and houses! Often the snow had a crust on it that would hold us up. At other times we would sink to our knees. We would stay outside until our feet were too cold to go on, our woolen snowsuits and mittens soaking wet. The cold, clear wind would blow across the fields; the blue-white snow and clear blue skies gave the land a beauty all its own.

By mid-March, Mainers begin to watch for spring, knowing that slush and mud are a part of winter's decline.

Pussy-willows lined the wet and swampy places. Grace and I would don our boots and go pussy-willowing to gather bunches of the long sprigs with the soft, silvery, little catkins lined up and down. When colored chalk came on the market, we would color them in pastels, but somehow I liked them in their natural silver color the best.

Another March tradition was tapping the maple trees. Two maples stood in the front yard. A hole was drilled in each and a spigot inserted, while Grandmother hung a bucket on the spigot and collected the sap. She would then pour the sap in a large shallow pan, which was set on the rear of the stove. The sap was gently simmered down from a clear liquid to the rich amber syrup that is so delicious to smother a biscuit with!

Apple blossoms and lilacs came in May in great profusion. An old orchard stood across the field and brook along the Griffin Road and berry bushes thrived back there also. It was a fun place to go and search out its treasures, and apple trees were usually very climbable for children. We girls would sit on the branches and sing, laugh and tell stories.

The fields in early summer were a profusion of wildflowers-buttercups, daisies, Indian Paintbrush. The meadowlarks would return and intrigue me with their songs. The barn would be opened and the barn swallows would swoop and dive in and out, their long forked tails and swift flights exciting to watch.

The banking boards that had been placed around the house's foundation, with fir tree branches underneath, were removed in spring and stacked up in the garage part of the shed. Since grandmother had no automobile, that area became my playhouse. The stack of banking boards held doll beds and dolls, and the room had other toys and a desk and slate where I could play school. Best of all, a swing hung down from the center and I could swing out the door! Over on one side stood an old sleigh with a bearskin lap robe in it. It was never taken out when I lived there, although I wished for it. My favorite summertime toy was a scooter with big wheels. I remember well pushing it and riding up and down the driveway on the only wheeled vehicle I ever owned as a child.

My cat was my pet and constant companion. It would follow me around, catch field mice, and, I'm sorry to say, an occasional bird. She would deposit them on the doorstep, and then lie very contentedly in the warm sunshine, always in my company.

We enjoyed the ephemeral summers to the fullest. Grandmother Griffin had a flower garden worthy of admiration, which neighbors and folks driving by often did. They would sometimes come into the yard to look more closely. I especially remember the tall purple larkspur as being my favorite. The flowers in the bed attracted butterflies and hummingbirds, which always interested me. There were groups of peonies in front of the side porch that always had tiny red ants on them, but the blooms were showy and colorful. We would sit on the porch in comfortable chairs, whenever we could on pleasant summer evenings.

Friends or neighbors would often drop by. If I was lucky, they would have a car with a rumble seat and take me for a ride! Or we would sit on the lawn with a pitcher of cold lemonade and homemade cookies providing a leisurely repast.

The highlight of summer was haying time. Mr. Libby would come down the road with mowers, hay rake, and wagons pulled by his horse, and then real activity would begin. It was so exciting to me! He brought helpers and I did all I could to get in the midst of it. I loved to ride in the wagon after they had filled it with hay and were heading to the barn. One day I saw a little dead snake in the hay. It dampened my spirits some, but not enough to give up riding the wagon! Sometimes Mr. Libby would set me up on the horse as it went back and forth up and down the drive working the pulley that unloaded the hay and dropped it through the high window into the haymows.

Now the big red barn had once stabled horses and cows too, I suppose, but when I lived there we had no stock; still it was an inviting place for children to explore. A rickety ladder went up one side of the hay mows to a VERY high catwalk across the barn to the other haymows. I had of course been cautioned not to ever attempt to climb up that ladder and to NEVER, EVER get on that catwalk. It provided an ever-present, scary challenge, one that I did on occasion accept, even though it WAS scary!

From the side porch we looked over the field across Griffin Road and to Mae Straw's house. Her family had lived there; she had not married, and now the house belonged to her. She was our nearest neighbor. Her house was smaller, white, with green shutters, the ever-present leafy elms along the roadside. She knew birds by sight and by their song. She loved wildflowers. One spring we watched goldfinches build their nest and raise their young in a lilac bush in front of a window. Mae would walk across her field with me to the Grove, as we called it. It had grand, tall fir trees, mossy places with Mayflowers, Lady Slippers, and Jack-in-the-Pulpits. It was a lovely quiet place. I would go there by myself and listen to the wind sing its special song through the fir trees. I was sad much later when it was all cut down to build Dow Field.

Mae had taught English at Bangor High School. She was retired, and I guess I was the only pupil who she could tell about nature and the Bible. She would read Bible stories to me and give me the prints of the wonderful old religious paintings. She would have me memorize some verses, like the Beatitudes and the 23rd Psalm. I have a New Testament she gave me in 1935 and a Green bird book dated 1938. She placed a sticker in the Testament under her signature that quotes Proverbs 4:23: "Keep thy heart with all diligence; for out of it are the issues of life." I feel that she adhered to this advice herself. Her living-room was cluttered with books and papers. I missed her after her death and I know Grandmother did. Her marker in Oak Grove Cemetery is a granite rock with a simple bronze plaque-somehow fitting to the lady who loved God and nature so.

Across the street from Mae Straw's house stood the original Griffin house. For a while, a family named Orr lived there. George Orr was the head of the house. He was friendly and neighborly as I recall. He must have had very big feet, though, because we would say that big shoes were as big as George Orr's overshoes! He had a little girl named

Cletye who would come and visit me sometimes. She gave me a big picture book that I kept for a long time. One summer day the news came that Cletye had drowned in nearby Kenduskeag Stream by the Bullseye Bridge. I had many sad thoughts about this lively little girl I had known so briefly, and who now was gone. Years later I found her grave in Maple Grove Cemetery. Her brother, Carlton Orr, was one of the first boys who left for World War II and his picture is in the serviceman's album in the Bangor Library.

The "Watkins Man' came in the summer, with his array of flavorings and spices. Purchases were made that were used in the delicious cookies and cakes baked in that iron stove oven, even through the hot summer! A bakery truck came by also, selling Drake's Cakes, breads, doughnuts, and wonderful-smelling packages of good things. Grandmother didn't purchase much from him, as she did her own baking, but she would indulge me with a Drake's Cake every now and then. Every child growing up in Bangor must have been intimately acquainted with yummy, cream-filled Drake's Cakes.

Most interesting of all, though, was a little thin woman in an old jalopy that would rattle into the driveway. I don't know who she was or where she came from, but she sold live chickens from that old car! Occasionally Grammie would purchase a hen to be baked. I never witnessed the "in-between" process. The wings of the hen would be used as light whisk brooms to brush crumbs or ashes away.

Chapter Three:

Living in the 30's

Often a passerby walking along the road would stop at the green pump over the artesian well by the barn. A dipper always hung there for anyone who needed a refreshing drink of cold water. We had to lug the drinking water into the house in big buckets. In winter we would sometimes need to prime the pump with hot water. A concrete cistern stood in the cellar to collect rainwater that was then pumped up into the black slate kitchen sink. It was usually heated in the stove tank or the kettle. The grey water was then poured down the sink into a covered trough that led to a ditch several feet behind the house. That grass along the ditch was always greener!

A big cupboard stood in the cellar which held home-canned vegetables, jams, jellies and homemade mincemeat. The vegetables came from a small garden that Grandmother tended behind the house; apples and berries came from the orchard. Potatoes and root crops were stored in another area on a dirt floor. The cellar could be entered either from the pantry or from the outside down some stone steps covered with cellar doors, the kind a child could slide down as in the old song "Playmate" (come out and play with me.)

In the summer of 1939 a terrific hurricane hit northern coastal New England. I recall my grandmother and I bracing ourselves, pushing against a door trying to close it against the unbelievable force of the wind. We suffered no damage, but I shall remember that fierce storm all my life. I was never afraid of thunderstorms; we two would often watch lightning in the skies and listen to thunder. It was part of the wonderment of nature.

The long shed between the house and the barn had an upstairs that we called the shed chamber. Such a treasure trove! Dozens of trunks and boxes contained old clothing, bonnets of sateen and ribbons, capes, skirts and dresses trimmed in laces and beading, fur muffs and stoles. A child's dress up dream! The boxes contained mostly books and keepsakes. Downstairs in the shed my father had a workshop with his familiar initials DRG on the door.

The attic in the house had a couple of trunks, some pieces of furniture, and a few odds and ends. Sometimes in winter Grandmother would carry washed clothes up there and hang them on lines. I would sometimes sit at the top of the stairs and speculate on a Morton's Salt poster that hung there with a picture of a girl in a yellow dress holding an umbrella in one hand and a box of salt in the other. That box in her hand had the same picture, and on and on to infinity? I wondered.

The second floor had four bedrooms. One had been converted to a kitchen with a little black stove and cupboards. Great Aunt Lizzie stayed there. She was Ella's sister who very tragically had lost her hearing and speech because of a childhood illness. She sat up there in a window and did perfectly beautiful handiwork-embroidery mostly. Not long after I came there she and my grandmother had a disagreement of some sort, and Lizzie left and spent the rest of her life in Pittsfield with a close friend named Mae Lane. Ella and Mae had been classmates at Maine CentralInstitute in Pittsfield. I would be driven to Mae's in the summer to spend a few days. We would do puzzles on her glassed in side porch. I would walk downtown to the 5 & 10 to spend a penny or so on candy. Mae's son Hollis and his wife lived in the house also. Some years ago I drove into the driveway of that rambling white house. It had a 'for sale' sign on it. Much to my surprise Hollis' widow still lived here, and she invited me in. It had not changed so much from what I remembered! I still have pleasant memories of that small town and those people.

Of course I would visit my other set of Grandparents, Grammie and Grampie Nickerson. Her name was Grace, and his was Albert. Grace had been raised at sea for the most part because her father was Captain James Nickels of Searsport. He was in the China trade and her varied stories of her life on shipboard and of faraway places mesmerized us girls. One story was about a stowaway boy whom she taught to read and write. Another was about a mischievous pet monkey that seemed to know who liked it and who didn't! Their ship even burned once going into Liverpool Harbor.

Grace went to great lengths to teach us manners-how to stand and sit up straight, and she tried to mold us into little ladies. Besides the three of us Griffin girls, there were two Nickerson girls, Natalie and Carolyn, or Kay, as we called her, and another two cousins, Irvin and Jimmy Wentworth. They were the cousins on mother's side of the family. Later, another cousin, Steve Nickerson, was born into the family.

Albert, who had been an engineer on the railroad, was seriously crippled with arthritis when we knew him well enough to remember him. He sat in his rocking chair with a tiered table by him that held his pipes, matches, ashtray, and tobacco. His joints were so terribly gnarled that we were a little afraid of him.

But the happiest days were at the farm. They were idyllic summer days- when the new-mown hay smelled sweet and luscious bowls of berries with fresh cream from the top of the milk bottle were on the table. We ran barefoot and drank the cool water from the well. The adult talk usually got around to war in those visits in the late 1930's. I remember asking Grandmother, "What is war?" She gave me to understand that it was great and terrible thing.

Another memorable event of those days was the explosion and burning of the dirigible Hindenburg, killing all on board. The Bangor Daily News had a picture of it. And a boy named Don Fendler was lost on Katahdin for eleven days. He survived on berries. Although a vigorous search was conducted, he walked out himself, not much the worse for wear!

Meanwhile, in September of 1935, Dudley remarried a widow with two daughters older than we were. Her name was Helen; she had lived next door to us, and had lost her husband to an illness about the same time our mother died. Her girls were named Ruth and Elizabeth. On the very cold New Year's Eve of 1937, Ruth was married in a home ceremony in Bangor. The living room chairs were pushed back. Dudley made a frame of chicken wire, laced it with fir boughs, and stood it in front of the windows. The dining room held the table with the wedding cake. Candles and ribbons adorned the rooms, and the bride and groom said their vows in front of the greenery. The big highlight for me was that I carried the train of the wedding dress down the staircase as the bride descended. Ruth wore a lovely satin dress with tiny covered buttons, and a juliette lace cap with a veil. Elizabeth, her maid of honor, wore a pale blue dress with a sweetheart neckline covered with sparkles. I thought it was all very beautiful! Grandmother had dressed me for the occasion in a green silk dress pinched together in front with three artificial flowers. My hair was introduced to the curling iron and a big bow was put on the back of my head. I had long white stockings over my long underwear and freshly polished Buster Brown shoes! It was my introduction to society! How delightful to participate in such a magical evening!

Griffin Family
Sons and daughter of Thomas and Asenath Wiley Griffin
(Back) Heman, Mason, Fred (grandfather)
(Front) Charles, Mary, George (circa 1900)

Family of Mary Griffin and Charles Merrill
Girls: Florence, Edith, Cicelia Boys: Tom, Sid, and (?)

Great Grandfather - Albion Dudley 1830-1907

Fred Griffin with his horses
Ella in chair - Union Street Farm

The Farm - southwest corner of Union Street and Griffin Road

Back of the Farm

Ella Dudley and Fred T. Griffin

A Social Club - 1911 - as named by Dudley Griffin
(Back row) Whit Whitermore, Millen, "Mac" McWilliams, Dudley, Dumpy Freeze, Slomy Tibbet
(Center) "Smoke" Clement, Fenno, Bob Hamilton, Dick House, Bug Bartlett, Willie Barker
(Front) "Admiral" Sawyer, "Skunk" Puton, "Deke" Robinson, Cliff Kenney, Minnie Mincher, "Square" Torrie

Dudley's cousin
Helen Dudley Eaton

Lois, Grandmother Griffin, Elinor (circa 1937)

Lois and Grace - winter at the Farm

Dudley Ralph Griffin

Mother - Louise Nickerson Graduated from E.M.G.H. Nursing School

Grace, Lois, Elinor (1940) at the Farm. Mae Straw's house in background

Great Grandfather - Capt. James N. Nickels
Searsport, Maine (1828-1889)

Capt. Nickels' daughters
Caroline, Grace (grandmother), Clara

One of Capt. Nickels' ships
The Oneida

Capt. Nickels' bark
The Moonbeam

Natalie Grace Waterhouse (Wentworth)
Capt. Nickels' grandaughter, Caroline's daughter

Jim and Irving Wentworth
(2nd cousins)

Louine Tibetts Huff
Grandaughter of Capt. Nickels

Brother and sister - Irving and Louise Nickerson

Natalie, Kay and Aunt Myrtle Nickerson

Cousins - Grace and Elinor Griffin
Natalie and Kay Nickerson

Elinor, Grace, Lois
A no-snow Christmas (1939)

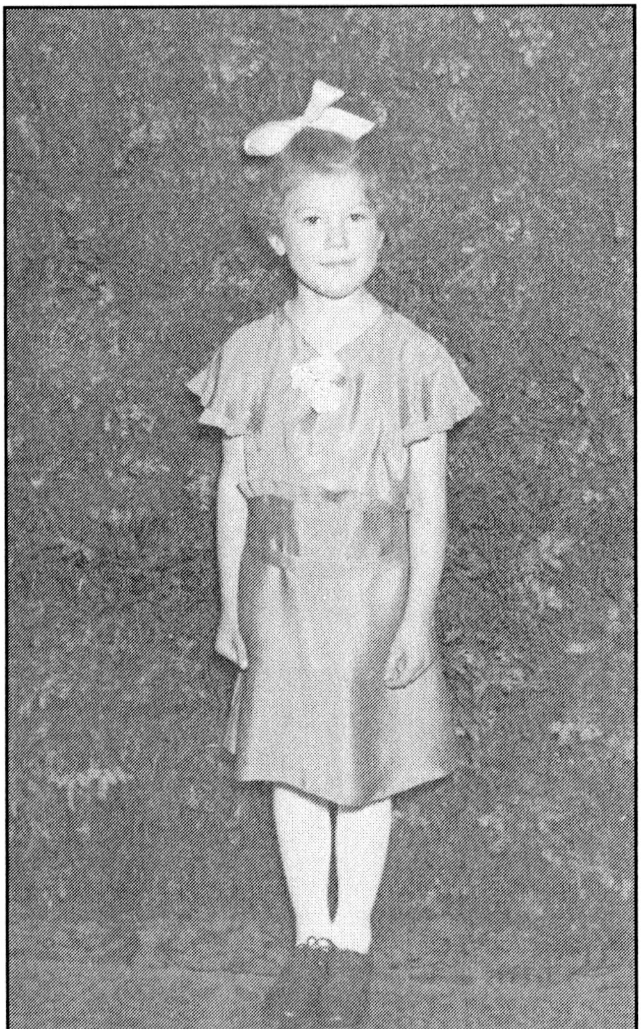

Lois at Ruth's New Year's Eve wedding

Chapter Four:

School

The Morrison family lived out Union Street from the farm. Ralph Morrison delivered milk to us in glass bottles which would have a paper cap on the top. In winter it would be pushed up by frozen milk above the bottle's neck. The cream, back then rose to the top and usually we would shake it up and mix it in with the milk. Sometimes though, we would pour some of the cream to use for something special, or to whip it with a hand-held and hand-powered beater! Any milk that happened to sour went to make a scrumptious chocolate cake.

The Morrison's' son, Alden, drove the school bus; he was the father of one of my playmates, Marjorie. We were on the bus from the beginning of the route when I began first grade at Fairmount School. Marjorie had a small playhouse in her yard with dolls and furniture. It was fun to be invited to her house to play. Her birthday was in July and for many years she had a birthday party. We played games and won prizes, and ate plenty of ice cream and Mrs. Morrison's delicious cakes. I remember that musical chairs was a favorite game.

After the school bus picked me up, we went across the Griffin Road to the Fuller Road, where we picked up the Clewley kids, among others. The Cram Road was on the route also. People said the Cram Road was crammed with holes (it probably was), and that the Fuller Road was full of ruts. We passed one nice little white house belonging to a lady named Maud Hunt. She was a friend of Grandmother's and she would sit on her porch in nice weather and wave at us.

At the end of the Cram Road was a house full of kids who would come running out to the bus. It was a novelty to me to be among all these children, but the family that appealed to me the most was the Treadwells at the corner of Griffin and Fuller Roads. They had four or five youngsters, and it seemed to me that they always had oodles of fun. They had so much fun that I wanted them to come to my house and play. My birthday, October 2nd, seemed to me to be a perfect time to invite them, and I had never had a birthday party. So, unbeknownst to my dear grandmother, I invited them to my house on that special day to celebrate with me. But the situation became really complicated when my father had me come to his house to a surprise party with my sisters and cousins. He had remarried by this time, and Helen had prepared the dining room table for a party, and she had baked a big birthday cake. They gave me a stuffed doll in plaid with a painted face, which I named Bubbles. But how I wished I were back at the farm with those Treadwells, for they had come, bringing hair ribbons for my gift. Grandmother rose to the occasion, however, and served them cake and other goodies, entertained them, and sent them home with something or other. One little girl received my green coat with a fur collar that I had barely outgrown! I don't recall the Treadwells ever coming to play with me at my house after that.

In Maine the school year begins the day after Labor Day. Folks who had moved out to their camps and cottages for the summer returned to town. Grammie Griffin kept me at home with her until first grade. You might say I was home schooled through kindergarten! So my first few days in school, sitting at a desk in a room full of other six- year-olds, were a bit unsettling! Our teacher was a matronly-looking lady named Miss Blanchard. During the year she became Mrs. Clark. I must have been completely overwhelmed on that first day as I went out into the hall and hollered for GRACE as loudly as I could! Grace's 6th grade teacher allowed her to go and see about her little sister! Poor Grace, a model of decorum, must have been mortified! I finally adjusted to the great adventure!

Those children who rode the school bus generally ate lunch at school. The others walked home for lunch and returned. My father had me walk to his house, where "dinner" was set on the table every day at 11:30. Supper was eaten in the evenings. So, I had time with my family each day, but still lived with my grandmother.

Among my new classmates was a little girl named Jean. Now she was an only child of adoring parents. Her hair was always curled, and she wore short, cute dresses and panties that matched and had patent leather shoes! I was my grandmother's child, with long stockings, Buster Brown shoes, and skirts discreetly over my knees. We could not have been dressed more unlike! But we were attracted to each other and were friends all through school. Her mom took us swimming, to ball games, and the like. We loved her, and she loved all of us girl friends.

We walked all over the neighborhood and got to know most of the people. We would often pause by the bakery on Hammond Street and smell the delicious odors emanating from within. Sometimes we would have enough change to go in and buy an éclair, often sharing it. There were two drugstores, Hawthorne's and Mishou's. We would look at magazines in Hawthorne's and buy a candy bar or chewing gum. Later Nancy Mishou became a classmate. How we loved to line up on the stools in front of the soda fountain at Mishou's and order root beer floats, chocolate malts, or butterscotch sundaes! Her parents generously made them for us, and we walked ALL the calories off! I cannot remember anyone being overweight then.

One incident that sticks in my mind occurred one day when I arrived at the farm after school, and my grandmother asked me what I had had for lunch. I told her about some wonderful chocolate pudding Helen had made, and how much I loved it. "Well," my grandmother said, "I can certainly make chocolate pudding." And make it she did! "But," I offered critically, "it's not satin smooth like Helen's." Whereupon Grammie, slightly disgusted, fumed "That's because hers is made from a box mix!"

I suppose it was a good thing that I was gently weaned away from my much-loved farm, and towards town and home there, for in July 1941, Grammie Griffin suffered a 'shock,' as they then called it or a stroke as it is known now. She lived only a couple weeks after that. My father and I had to go around to each of the neighbors to tell them of her death. I wept bitter tears, when I lost her and my home. I went around the big old house, shed, and barn, rubbing my hands on things, kissing some of them good-bye. The funeral service was held at the house. People came and went, and flowers seemed to be everywhere. The door closed that day on that part of my life but I still remember the rooms, the fields and trees, and the strong quiet lady that took on the rearing of a headstrong little girl.

Within a year's time, the United States Government purchased the farmland, including Mae Straw's, and Dow Field was built. In a way it was a blessing that those two women did not live to see their homes demolished, the grove and orchard leveled and fenced off and runways built. Now when I fly into Bangor and the plane lands on the very spot where I lived and played, I remember it as it was, and with great happiness I step off the plane onto home ground.

Chapter Five:

Back Home and the War Years

Life for me became very different, as I was now part of a household with my two older sisters, my father and my stepmother. A stepsister with a baby boy lived next door. There were no longer fields to roam but, there was an apple tree that was exceptionally good to climb, a pear tree that blossomed outside my bedroom window, and a back yard with Appalachian lawn chairs and a homemade fireplace. Daddy strung colored lights across the yard, and we spent many happy hours there with friends and neighbors. A lawn on one side of the house was perfect for croquet. One corner out back was tilled and planted with our Victory Garden. We would have had a vegetable garden anyway, but everyone during those war years was urged to grow all they could. They were called Victory Gardens. We grew string beans, carrots, tomatoes, cucumbers, radishes, lettuce and gladiolas! My father loved those tall showy flowers, and the outside edge of our plot was lined with their blossoms. Helen canned beans, put up apples and pears, and made pickles. We had a cherry tree, but the birds nearly always got to those before we did! Nearly everyone I knew had a little clump of rhubarb. We youngsters would pick the tender shoots and salt and eat them, and then we would make faces because they were so sour!

Of course, there were no supermarkets then. Each neighborhood had its own small grocery store. Ours was Harry Baker's, on Bowdin Street, only a block away. We could take a shortcut through the neighbor's yard across the street, or walk halfway around the block to reach it, chatting with neighbors along the way. I often went to get a loaf of bread (10 cents), a pound of hamburger (freshly ground while you waited, 25 cents a pound), and fresh eggs that a clerk, Don Bell, often drew faces on! The store had a big walkin icebox with windows, and you could view the meats, cheeses, milk and cream, skinless hotdogs, and redskins. If I was lucky I'd have a penny for a piece of candy or bubblegum. A nickel would buy some Necco wafers, licorice, or a Drake's Cake!

Everyone had iceboxes in the '30's and early '40's. Ours sat out in the shed by the back door. (Sheds are now more euphemistically called mud rooms.) One compartment in the icebox was lined with zinc, and a block of ice sat in it and kept the other compartments cool. Getchell Ice Company had trucks loaded with blocks of ice and they would make their runs through the neighborhoods. Each household had an ice card. They placed it in a front window when they needed ice. Depending on whether they needed a 10, 25, or 50-pound chunk, they would place the card on its side, upside down, or right side up.

Some of the high school boys worked on the ice

trucks in the summer. They would put a big piece of leather over one shoulder, pick up the ice with big tongs, sling it up on their shoulder, and carry it up to the house and put it in the icebox. We children would run out to the ice truck and get the small pieces of ice that had been chunked out with an ice pick so the tongs would hold. Ice was stored in ice houses and packed in sawdust. In winter, of course, there was no need for ice delivery. We got an electric refrigerator about the time the war ended and ice boxes became popular only in antique malls!

I had a nice bedroom with my things scattered around. Grandmother Griffin's desk, which I had seen her sit at and write letters many, many times, was part of the furnishings. I have kept it all these years and done much correspondence on it. My oldest sister, Elinor, had a great room on the third floor. It was colorful, and had built-in bookshelves and a big closet. Grace and I liked to go up to her room at night and look down into the street through the leafy shadows of the big trees out front. During Fair time we could watch the fireworks from there. In winter the stark beauty of the snowy landscape glistened through the glow of a street light.

Elinor had our mother's cedar chest in her room. Sometimes I would look at the things in it that had belonged to our mother wondering about this woman who had given birth to me. Her nursing school pictures, a diary in which she wrote after I was born, a silk turquoise kimono, fringed in black and other personal items. Most fascinating was s ship's log from the ship Alameda that Grandmother Nickerson had kept. Much of it could be read, but most of it had been pasted over with recipes and poetry. It is now in a cousin's possession. In a letter written by Captain Nickels from LeHavre on July 20, 1882, he proudly admits to Callie (his daughter Caroline), that "we beat every ship coming from San Francisco except two".

A colorful story of Captain Nickels tells of him commanding the Brig. Waccamaw, and sailing into Searsport Harbor flying the Confederate flag. His papers had been confiscated by the Collector of Customs in South Carolina in 1861, the onset of the Civil War. He flew the Stars and Bars through the Blockade, probably the only time the Confederate flag was ever flown into Penobscot Bay. He commanded six ships from 1861 to 1887. I think he must have been a colorful man with a commanding presence.

The outer attic room held Grammie Griffin's old Victrola, which had been in her dining room on the farm. Elinor loved music and had a lovely voice. Deanna Durbin records were played often along with a couple of old World War I songs. "My Sweetheart is somewhere in France", and another I cannot recall. But we would wind up that old Victrola with the crank on the side, and play records for hours.

When senior prom time came, Elinor was upstairs getting ready to go when her date arrived at the front door. He turned the handle on the doorbell in the center of the door and it made a loud BRRRING. I ran to answer the door. He stood there very handsomely. I said "She'll be down in a minute,", and promptly shut the door! The poor guy had to stand there on the front steps until someone let him in. Well, another lesson in social graces learned that night!

I was playing in the house that December 7, 1941, when the news of Pearl Harbor came over the radio. My parents were in the living room listening. The radio was certainly a central part of our lives then. For the next few years we could easily recognize the voices of Edward R. Murrow, Walter Winchell ("Good morning, Mr. and Mrs. America and all the ships at sea; let's go to press"), H.V. Kaltenborn, and Bob Trout, because we depended on them for news reports and war stories. Life magazine, with its wonderful photography, brought some of the reality of war into our home. The movie theater always carried some photo footage from the front lines in their newsreel.

Radio entertainment was provided by comedians like Jack Benny, Fred Allen, and Fibber McGee and Molly. Upstairs we girls had a radio in Grace's room. We listened to music like "Your Hit Parade," the top songs of the week, "The Chesterfield Hour," Johnny Mercer, Francis Langford, and a blue-eyed boy on the block named Frank Sinatra. Elinor loved opera and would listen to the Texaco opera broadcast on Saturdays. All of us liked "The Firestone Hour," and the Longine's Watch hour, which featured beautiful classical and semi-classical music.

Books were also an integral part of life. We girls read poetry and prose aloud to each other. Bangor's Carnegie Library was, and is, outstanding, and we took advantage of it; we were all avid readers.

The move into town put me into a different school zone, and I was transferred to Hanibal Hamlin, named for Lincoln's first vice president. Hamlin was a Mainer and had a home on Hammond Street. The school was an old brick building at the intersection of Union, Hammond, and 4th Streets. It had a fire escape on one side of the school and a small building to one side. Voting took place in the smaller building, but only by Maine citizens who had paid their poll tax. My father had attended school in the old building, and it must have been really old because my father was born in 1891. It had hardwood floors and creaky stairs, worn by the footsteps of hundreds of children's feet. 'Lefty" Grant was the principal and he also taught part of the 6th grade classes. I was there for 4th, 5th, and 6th grades.

Each week we had the opportunity to purchase defense stamps. We saved our money and bought as many as we could of the 10-cent, 25-cent, or $1.00 stamps. When we filled a book it was worth $18.75, which could be redeemed after the war. Everything was for the war effort. We saved every tidbit of tin foil, string, and grease. We would cut the tops and bottoms out of tin cans and stomp them flat. Gasoline, meat, and sugar were all rationed. Adults had just so many coupons they could acquire these things with. Each family with someone in any branch of the service hung a small flag with a blue star in their window. Sadly, we saw some of them replaced with a gold star, which meant that serviceman had given his life for his country and would not be returning home.

My father, an electrician, worked on the development of Dow Field. He did the wiring for the runway lights along with the tower. All the workers worked overtime. Very soon the air corps personnel were there along with the planes. The P-38's were wonderment and everyone came out to see them.

At Hanibal Hamlin School during the Christmas season, a huge tree was set up and decorated, and all the students gathered to sing Christmas carols and remember our servicemen and women. The war years made a lasting impression on all of us. In all our homes we had blackout curtains. When a siren went off for a blackout drill, we gathered in the kitchen where our curtains were. All the lights in the city were turned out and everything was dark. Harry Baker was our neighborhood warden; he walked around to make sure not one little glimmer of light was showing. This was practice in the event German war planes should ever darken our skies. The Civilian Air Patrol flew along the coastline. U-Boats did come close to Maine shores. One night two German spies were put ashore at Hancock Point, and we were all watchful.

Dudley & Helen with her children and their spouses;
Ruth, Dudley, Ray, Helen, Bob, Libby

Ruth - stepsister

Elizabeth - stepsister

Brian Grant, Polly Pugsley, Julie and Sue Grant
Stepnephew and nieces - one missing, Pricilla

Lois, Grace, Elinor with 2 stepsisters
Ruth Robinson Grant and Elizabeth Robinson Pugsley

Chapter Six:

Family Folks

When Dow Field was completed, my father was asked to go to the Brunswick Naval Air Station and do the same work. He and Helen decided they would go to Lewiston and stay with her mother and he could commute to Brunswick. By this time, Elinor was in Boston in nursing school. She had joined the Cadet Nurse Corps and received her training. Grace and I were boarded at Aunt Helen Eaton's. She was Dad's first cousin, and lived diagonally across on West Broadway. She and her husband Herbert had a large house, and she had space for us, a woman and her daughter, and the young wife of a serviceman from Waverly, New York. Grace and I were not too happy about the situation, but everyone did what they could for the war effort! Aunt Helen was very gregarious, with a vigorous approach to life. Later she had a guest house in Freeport, similar to what we now call "Bed and Breakfast" homes.

Sometimes Grace and I went to Bangor's wonderful old stone depot and took the Yankee Flyer train to Lewiston. We also stayed at Grammie Dudley's. She was no relation to my own grandmother, Ella Dudley Griffin; she was Helen's mother, and we had good times with her. She was a businesswoman, with a wholesale greeting card company. What absolute fun it was to cruise through her shop and stockroom! Besides cards, stationery, wrapping paper, and school supplies, there were games, puzzles, dolls, and toys. She loved going to New York on buying trips, and she always took in the latest Broadway show. She liked music, and had the first record player I ever saw where a stack of records could be put on and it would automatically change them. She would give us money to go out and buy for her. Fred Waring and his Pennsylvanians were a favorite of us both. She liked to eat in nice places-the white tablecloth kind, and I thought it was wonderful!

Libby, Helen's second daughter, lived in a third floor apartment in Grammie Dudley's big house. She had married on a Thanksgiving in a lovely home ceremony. Her husband was overseas in the Army, and Libby had a baby girl to care for. One feature of the house was a dumb-waiter that we could send things all the way from downstairs to her apartment. Its original function was to send things that needed to be cool down to the cellar.

Summer brought the end of construction for Dad in Brunswick, and we all returned home to Bangor. Elinor would come home for holidays and vacations to her aerie on the third floor. She was a demanding individual with definite ideas, and gave advice freely to me, which I rebuffed if possible! Not until I reached adulthood did I appreciate the really deep love and loyalty that she held for her family and friends. She had a real joie de vivre.

Grace graduated from Bangor High in 1944 and went to the University of Maine. She could knit and study at the same time! She picked a pattern once for a sweater of two shades of blue that I thought was ugly until it was finished! Then I changed my tune and borrowed it whenever I could. I liked to take the bus up to Orono and visit her. She had a lot of great friends, and they would invite me to go to Pat's Pizza with them-THE off-campus hangout for students! She was president of Phi Mu sorority her senior year.

Since my father was an only child, we had no first cousins on his side. My mother had one brother named Uncle Irvin Nickerson, whom we adored. He was very tall (6'4"), and lean, graceful, musical, and full of fun. He and Aunt Myrtle were a tremendous help to Dad when Mother died. They had two daughters who were seemingly opposite in personalities, Natalie and Carolyn (Kay). Natalie liked to direct the show and keep all of her ducks in a neat row while Kay had a gentle heart that embraced all far and wide. Natalie and Elinor were about the same age, and although they were close in their kinship they could have real arguments! I don't believe Kay ever really argued with anyone. She spent her summers with her grandmother on her farm. She spoke horse language and as she rode she and the horse became one. Kay with the gentle heart was never without an assortment of pets to love.

Uncle Irvin had a second marriage to Eva, a wonderful woman with several children but she and Uncle Irvin soon conceived one of their own and named him Steve. I baby-sat him sometimes. One time one of her older sons was home from the hospital where he was undergoing extensive skin grafts. He had been on an oil tanker at Pearl Harbor and was burned terribly. His scars made a big impression on me and I hardly knew what to say to him. Uncle Irvin worked for the Fro-Joy ice cream factory, which was on Pier Street and 6th Street, an easy walk from our house. Irvin managed it at night, so on many evenings Daddy would suggest ice cream and we would willingly go to the ice cream factory! Sometimes we would get a tour and go into the huge freezer and select ice cream bars, pushups, and other frozen delights. It was a wonderful treat and we were always welcomed by our uncle and co-workers.

Our two second cousins were named Irvin and Jim. Irvin was the oldest of all of us, while Jim was Kay's age. We all had the same great-grandfather, Captain James Nichels of Searsport. We would gather for outings in Orrington at Aunt Sue's summer place on a cliff overlooking the Penobscot River. Sue and Louine, two more second cousins, were middle-aged sisters who were granddaughters of Captain Nickels who had three girls. His only son died and was buried at sea as a boy. We called them both aunts. Their mother was Clara. Sue's summer house was next to the Dean Cemetery, and separated from it by a thick cedar hedge. We children had great fun playing hide-and-go seek in and out of that hedge and around the headstones in the cemetery. Jim would give some of us bumpy rides in Sue's wheelbarrow. Arthur Pierce, Sue's husband, had a big bell mounted in the yard. They would ring when a certain boat came up or down the river, and the boat would toot back.

We called Sue and Louine's father "Uncle Doctor", as he was Dr. Tibbetts. Sue became a nurse and Louine was a medical secretary to Surgeon Generals at Walter Reed Hospital for years. Jim and Irvin's mother, Natalie Grace (Aunt Nat), was a nurse also, as was my own mother. Aunt Nat was the school nurse when I was in grade school. She was part of a team that checked our eyesight, weight, tonsils, and small illnesses. I always dreaded it because I had large tonsils and she used to say they needed to come out, which frightened me to death! I managed to avoid that bit of surgery all of the years I was growing up. The story of Aunt Nat's parents is tragic. Caroline McGilvery Nickels had been born at sea, March, 1867, on the Bark McGilvery. She attended Farmington Normal School and married a sea captain in 1888, one James Y. Waterhouse. Poignant correspondence remains written as he lay very ill with a leg injury in Portland, Maine's General Hospital. She apparently had consumption, as he worried about her health. She gave birth to a daughter while at Farmington, Grace Natalie. James died of his injury and his father-in-law, Captain Nickels, went to Portland to make funeral arrangements. This accomplished, he went into a restaurant to get supper. While there he fell from his chair and died immediately of a heart attack. The remains of Captain Nickels and Captain Waterhouse arrived back in Searsport together in April, 1889. Caroline died in her 27th year in 1894. Grace Natalie went to live with her Aunt Grace Nickerson, my grandmother.

Daddy's first cousin, Helen Eaton, had two grandchildren, Laurel Ann and Eaton Robinson, who came every summer from Freeport for visits. She would happily take me, along with Laurel and Eaton, to Hershey's Retreat at Sandy Point for a week. The retreat belonged to the Universalist Church, which we attended, and in the summer different groups from church would spend time there. It was situated on a point on Penobscot Bay, a beautiful setting, which I hardly appreciated then. We played croquet, waded in the cold Atlantic, walked to a nearby store for ice cream, and played games on the piazza that ran across the front of the mansion. Adults played cards and sat in the rockers and enjoyed the view. It was nice, but I never really loved going there.

Helen Eaton was outgoing and fun-loving and liked to include any of us youngsters in activities. She would cook eels, which I never ever tasted, thank you very much! She had a big dog named Andy- white with a speckled nose, perhaps part setter. He had a silky coat and I loved him. My father did not like dogs, so we never had one, but wegirls all grew up to be dog lovers. Helen Eaton's husband, Herbert, was a man of few words. He just smoked his pipe and thought for a long time before he ever gave a comment or answered a question.

When I was small, Dad and Helen rented a cottage each summer for a few weeks. We went to Pushaw Pond, which Grace and I didn't care for because the bottom was mucky. We also went to Northport twice because it was close to Belfast where Helen's brother and his family lived. We had great fun hiking around, going out on the pier, watching the sailboat races, and exploring the shore. My, but the salt water was cold! We would stay in it until we were blue! There was a small store near the cabins and a daily trip to the candy counter was eagerly anticipated. I remember asking for a sucker one day. The owner asked me what color, and when I replied that it didn't really matter, he exclaimed that I was a girl after his own heart-not too fussy! We always had fun as our two families were combined and as I got to know my two stepsisters and their husbands, also Helen's brother, his wife and their three children in Belfast. They were the Stone family.

Chapter Seven:

Camp

After the farm was sold, Dad bought an old log camp on Phillips Lake. It necessitated a lot or work, which suited him fine, since work was his avocation also. He leveled the floors, built a new staircase inside, and otherwise generally fixed it up. He worked on it as long as he had it. We could not drive directly to it, so either parked at the top of a hill and walked down a woody path to it, or parked over at Dailey's Beach and walked the railroad tracks to it. The tracks were immediately behind the camp, and when the trains went by boy, did it shake us! We used to put pennies on the tracks to see them flattened out. Although railroad ties are not spaced to make walking easy, we walked for miles up and down the tracks.

An assortment of painted chairs adorned the yard and the front porch. On delightful evenings we would sit on the porch, eat supper and watch glorious sunsets over Chase Mountain.

Dad built a rowboat and, not satisfied with it, he then bought one. I loved to row, and I rowed all around the narrow end of the lake. We had a 5 1/2 hp Johnson motor for it too. Rocks sticking above the water out front were perfect to swim out to, dive from and sit on. I knew a place across the lake where a whole field of pink ladies' slippers grew in spring. Exploring the woods always brought wonderful surprises. For example, I really loved the ferns, lichen and moss covered rocks. One camp across the lake had an appealing small gravestone engraved "Here lies Mike, a damn good cat"! A succinct description, for sure! Down from that camp were the remains of some wonderful old log cabins and a lodge with a huge fieldstone fireplace. It was known around the lake as "The Teacher's Colony." It was said to have been built for artists and educators to come to in the summer for enrichment. It had not succeeded, and animals had ravaged the wood floors, people had carried off the doors and windows, and eventually I suppose it fell in.

My father liked to hike in the woods and I was a very willing and enthusiastic partner. We walked up the mountain across from camp to the remains of the cellar of a house surrounded by scrubby apple trees. We tramped up the other side, north of Route 1A to Sunset Rock, and explored forest roads; we found remains of saunas, which are small log huts filled with rocks. We found out that a settlement of Finnish people had come to the area. I had a couple of girl friends whose families had cottages at the Lucerne end, and I would often go down there. I knew the lake and it sislands quite well.

We would hike up Bald Mountain, climb the fire tower, and admire the view, pick blueberries to take back for blueberry pies, pancakes, or just to eat. Wild Maine berries are wonderfully sweet and tasty. We drew our drinking water from a well, or we went up the lake to a spring that ran clear and cold. My, that was good water! Generally we would take the boat up past Dailey's Beach to the spring, fill our jugs and then come back.

One winter, when I was a sophomore at Bangor High, our basketball team won the state tournament. It was very exciting! We had watched all the home games in the big old yellow frame auditorium on Main Street. Of course, we would have loved to have gone to Boston to the New England championship games (B.H.S. lost to Fall River, Massachusetts.) We all thought they should cancel school, since so many students had gone with the team and the cheerleaders, but they didn't. Four or five of us girls decided we would skip school and go down to my camp. Jean could drive so she got her mother's car and we bought the makings for spaghetti. I commandeered the key to the camp, and off we went. There was snow and ice, which added to both the novelty and the beauty. We built a wood fire and set the sauce to simmering, while we ran around over the frozen lake, played card games, and generally amused ourselves! I think I remember that we got caught, but we created a good memory that was savored by the participants for years and years.

Dad carried a big red knapsack on his back with supplies in it as he trekked back and forth to the camp. He had carried it for years through many camping adventures. Sometimes he would even put live lobsters in it for a lobster feed on the lake. On the 4th of July we usually had lots of people over for the traditional salmon and fresh English peas. I loved it when others came, for we always had good times. Helen's grandchildren came often, especially the three in Hampden. The oldest was a boy, Brian, whom Dad enjoyed very much. Julie and Sue were lively and always seemed to have fun there also. Libby and Bob, in Lewiston, had Polly and Priscilla. They would come and spend time too.

How lucky we were to have a place on the water that we could go and have so much fun at with friends and relatives. I shall never forget swimming on the moonlight "path" at night, stars over the lake, fireworks on the 4th, long walks, listening to the rain on the roof, snuggling under a quilt and sleeping soundly, even not hearing the trains go by! Those memories are dear to my heart.

Chapter Eight:

Bangor

After I had come to town to live, my father took me to join Brownie Scouts. The troop met at the Children's Home in the shadow of The Standpipe on Thomas Hill. The leader of the troop was Gertrude Campbell, known as "Tawny". She was an outstanding woman, and she led scouting and Camp Natarswi to great heights. She later became the national executive director of Girl Scouts in New York. We had some girls in our troop who lived at the orphanage. I was fascinated by what I perceived as dorm living, and I wondered about their parents.

The white Standpipe, a water reservoir, was painted olive green during the war years to camouflage it, and was closed to visitors. It was returned to its white color after the war ended, and the landmark stands thusly today.

In the immediate neighborhood of my home, I had several playmates, mostly boys. I had a bat and a black taped baseball. We played ball in the middle of the street and kick the can on summer evenings. One summer we thought we would do something nice for the Air Corp guys at Dow Field. We cleaned up a garage, created a stage from banking boards, arranged chairs facing them, and rehearsed some parts we had decided upon to entertain the troops. I was to sing "Send Her One Dozen Roses" in my inimitable tuneless fashion. Poems were memorized, skits put together, and we were ready! We went up on Hammond Street, and every time a soldier came by we invited him to come to our entertainment. Surprise, surprise! We had no takers! But we got someone's garage cleaned up, and it kept us busy for awhile.

Of course we all walked back and forth to school. We would meet friends along the way and everybody always had lots to talk about. First a girl named Alice, with thick dark hair that her mother fixed in lovely curls, then Marilyn, Eleanor and more. In winter after a new snow, we would put down our books and make snow angels on the bank by the Hanibal Hamlin house. We had a hill to climb when we came home, and two hills when we walked from high school.

We sisters walked up State Street every Friday afternoon when Grandmother Nickerson was alive. She was living in the Old Ladies' Home. We visited her each week, often riding back home on the noisy, clanging, old trolley car, which could be driven from either end. It was hooked to the electricity overhead by a cable that shot off sparks from time to time. When buses were introduced they were quiet and could be boarded from the curb rather than the middle of the street, but they were never as colorful as the old trolley!

The Vafiades family made Italian sandwiches in their store on Hammond Street. We loved those sandwiches. We would also stand outside the bakery next door and try to decide between buying a cream puff, an éclair, or some other delicious item. However, the winner for the best Italian anywhere was, and is, The Coffeepot. Thankfully it is one of the few places in Bangor that remains ever the same.

Sometimes we would plead with our father to take us to The Auto Rest and sometimes he would oblige! Local folks could while away a Sunday afternoon by driving about 15 miles west on Route 2 to Carmel to a sort of mini-amusement park. A black bear paced in a cage, deer grazed in a fenced-in area, and peacocks strutted around with their gorgeous plumage. We could eat a hotdog, or some pop-corn or ice cream and ride a merry-go-round. Later when we were in high school we went to some barn dances there.

When we were very young girls, we would walk downtown and buy paper dolls at J.J. Newberry's or F. W. Woolworth's 5 & 10 cent store. The last of April the counters were full of pastel colored May baskets. They were frilly and ruffly. We would fill them with small pastel candies and on May First (May Day), we would hang a basket on the doors of our best friends. As we got older we would go to Freeze's, Bangor's only real department store and look at merchandise. We would get on the elevator on the first floor, the operator would close the iron gate, push the buttons and up we'd go. I liked to walk down the wide, creaky, wooden steps and look out over the floors, especially at Christmas time when decorations were put up. I remember after the war when Freeze's had nylon stocking sales. A horde of women and girls would wait at the door, and when it opened we would rush in to buy nylons. A vast improvement over silk and cotton stockings! We would go to Frawley's Drug Store, or Sweets, or a place on the corner of Hammond and Main Streets that I cannot recall the name of now. All drug stores had soda fountains. Milkshakes, gooey sundaes, root beer floats, cherry cokes-only our decision on which was difficult to make.

As we girls grew older we loved to shop in some of the nicer stores. R.H. Rhines carried Knobby-Knit sweaters when they were in vogue. Burdell's and Cortell-Seagels were favorites for a formal dress, or otherwise nice outfit.

We Griffin girls purchased shoes at the Standard Shoe Store and had Ernie Shiro wait on us. This was at the behest of Dad who wanted us shod in sensible shoes. Saddle shoes and penny loafers were popular.

Usually if a good movie was playing at the Opera House on Maine Street or at the Bijou Theater on Exchange Street, one would attend on Sunday afternoon. Many of the wartime films were excellent, with good acting. The newsreels we watched with great attentiveness. They were all we could see of the war, outside of Life magazine whose pictures we pored over. My friend, Sally, and I went to see an unforgettable tragically sad movie when we saw the true story of the Sullivan brothers. Five brothers, who grew up in a town in Iowa, joined the Navy in January, 1942. They had always been very close, and requested the Navy to allow them to serve on the same ship. So all five were aboard the U.S.S. Juneau when it was blown up in November of 1942. The Navy changed their policy after that, and would not put brothers on the same ship. We wept for the boys and their parents who lost all of their sons.

W.C. Bryant's at 46 Main Street was the venerable old jewelry store where brides- to-be registered for fine china, crystal, and silver. When they wore a diamond it probably came from there. Of course Freeze's had lovely gifts also. My senior year in high school I worked at Bryant's during Christmas holidays. I loved the beautiful things and I learned a great deal about them.

I had done baby-sitting for three or four different families, but this was the first time I worked with the public. I enjoyed the experience, but sales were not my forte!

Malls are so very different from downtown Main Street in a small city or town. I'm glad I knew Bangor when an assortment of stores lined Main Street. Dakin's Sporting Goods was close by and Utterbacks, where one purchased luggage and leather goods.

City Hall stood on the corner of Hammond and Columbia Streets. Bangor High School held junior exhibitions there. Musical performances were given and John Bapst High School held coffee parties. These were bazaars of a sort to raise money for the Catholic school. I bought a chance and won a green wool blanket, the first thing I ever won!

Further down the block on Columbia Street was Lufkins Candy Shop. Mouth watering confections filled their shelves, not the least of which was the salt water taffy. Off Columbia, on Middle Street, was a restaurant with wonderful food. It was called "Ye Olde House," and was run by George and Vinette MacLeod, friends of my parents. On Thursdays they served the New England boiled dinner; corned beef and cabbage, and other vegetables. It was my favorite!

Across the street from the Hanibal Hamlin house is the Bangor Theological Seminary, with lovely tall trees and a hill that we sometimes slid down in winter. Mostly we went sledding down 6th Street, behind the ice cream factory. It would be blocked off for us, and we spent hours sliding down and pulling our sleds back up just to sled down again. One of my friends lived on 6th Street, and her mother often would make hot chocolate for us.

When I went to 7th grade and Fifth Street Junior High, I was reunited with friends from earlier years at Fairmount. It was great fun to grow up in an area where you knew almost everyone, had lots of friends, and could walk all around the neighborhoods and feel perfectly safe. My parents decided it was time for dancing and social graces when I entered 7th grade, so I was enrolled in Polly Thomas' Dancing School along with many of my friends. The lessons took place in a wonderful old house on Union Street, known as the Farrar House or the Symphony House. After we mastered (supposedly) the steps of the waltz, the fox trot, and a little jitterbugging, we were to have a dance and box supper. I invited a boy named David Finnegan. Because I had a penchant for being places on time, or even a bit early, I told him to come at a time that was 30 minutes sooner than it needed to be. Apparently he also believed in timeliness, for he came 30 minutes before I told him! But I was ready and waiting in a purple dress with an accordion pleated skirt that had been Grace's, and a pair of black suede shoes. We walked to the dance with the box supper which I had prepared. I made olive butter sandwiches, and I wondered if he would like them. He politely ate them anyway and I never did find out whether he liked olive butter or not. And of course we were there ahead of anyone else!

Later, in 8th or 9th grade, we had a formal, my first. Helen made me a pretty turquoise dress with tiny white flowers on it. It had a square neckline and a gathered skirt. A cute, vivacious boy named Forrest invited me to go with him. He sent me a corsage of yellow rosebuds and his father picked us up and drove us to the dance. After the dance was over, we walked home. A song called "Let's Take the Long Way Home" was popular then, and many couples thought it was a grand idea. It's really nice when the world is young, the evening warm and lovely, and innocence prevails!

Later in high school there were many sorority and club dances. All of us girls wore formals and the boys had suits or sport coats. We danced mostly to Nat Diamond's music at the Bangor House or Penobscot Valley Country Club. The girls wore"bids" on their wrists, with the dances numbered, and boys could sign them for different dances with the girl who wore that bid. I don't recall if it always worked just that way, but it was a nice idea! The girls wore corsages: sweet, sweet gardenias, sometimes an orchid or roses. The boys would have their parents' car; families in those days generally had only one car! Afterward we would usually eat at Pilot's Grill, opposite Dow Field. For a little while a hamburger stand opened up beside Pilot's, called Co-Pilots. They had wonderful hamburgers- perhaps too good, because the Co-Pilot idea, I believe, didn't suit Pilot's too well and it closed. Before one formal, a girl named Kay had a dessert party. About a dozen of us with our dates were invited to her home, where scrumptious desserts were served. A picture of all of us was taken. It was a lovely party. "Good Nigh Sweetheart" ended the dances, and it was all very much fun.

Between Webber Oil Co. and the church on Hammond Street was a white house curtained with newspapers. We children considered the woman who lived there by herself to be a funny little old lady. She wore men's clothes, and we heard that they had been her dead husband's! Her house was a target for pranks on Halloween; her windows were soaped, clotheslines were cut, and any number of things were done to that house. I think Elinor and her friends had the hose turned on them one year. I think they left her alone from then on! We called her Grammie Pickle. I don't know if that was her real name or not, and she remained a mystery to me.

In the fall of 1947 the town and surrounding area of Bar Harbor burned. The glow was visible as far as 30 miles inland to Bangor. The wind brought the smoke to us and we smelled it for days with the terrible fire that ravaged the area. Some of the older boys went to the island of Mt. Desert to help fight the blazes that destroyed many millionaires' summer homes. Edward Herlihy, a pre-med student at Bowdoin College, along with three other boys, was killed in an auto accident on their way back to school after days of fire-fighting. It struck a very sad note in Bangor. The Herlihy family was very well respected and loved. His father was our family physician, and his sister, Mary Ellen and I became friends at Camp Natarswi.

One of Dad's cousins, Celia Merrill, was married to King Elridge. They operated Oak Point Lobster Pound in Trenton. We had wonderful clam bakes on the shore there; steamers, lobster and corn-on-the-cob. I don't remember ever not loving clams and lobster!

I would go with Dad to visit Celia's sister, Edith Hershey, and her husband Guy, who lived on Plaisted Street. Dad was good to visit and keep in touch with relatives and old friends.

Dad's Aunt Mary, the one daughter of Asenath and Thomas Griffin had marred a Merrill. They had three daughters and four sons. Celia and Edith are the only two I remember.

Chapter Nine:

Natarswi

Camp Natarswi, the Abnaki Girl Scout Council's summer camp, was 18 miles on a dirt road beyond Millinocket on Togue Pond. It had what has to be the most perfect view of Mt. Katahdin sitting majestically over it. The log buildings were erected by the CCC (Civilian Conservation Corps) in the 1930's. Cyr buses picked us up in the parking lot across from B.H.S on Harlow Street. We would load our gear (one trunk and one duffle bag) and off we would go for the long, jostling ride, singing, laughing, and talking all the way.

In 1941 a forest fire had burned much of the acreage around Natarswi. The first summer I went up there in 1942 it was a scarred land, but Mainers know that a burn means wild, sweet blueberries would be plentiful! Many times while at camp we had to have a cup of blueberries to be admitted to the dining hall. We were well rewarded with blueberry pancakes or muffins.

The youngest campers were put in a long log cabin beside the dining hall. Of course, there were no amenities as we know them today. No electricity and no running water. A pump supplied our only drinking water. Later, as we got older, we lived in floored tents- five girls to each tent. We always had an orange crate by our beds to put things on.

Tawny was the camp director the first few years I was there. She was wonderful in her role and all the girls loved her. When the gong sounded for mealtimes we would line up by units in front of the dining hall. Tawny would stand up on the little porch, knitting on a yellow sock. We would kid her about the yellow sock, as she was always taking it out and redoing it. It was a clever ploy that she used and we all had a good time with it as we waited in line. Each unit entered and sat at long picnic tables. Each table had a "hopper," who hopped up to get extra helpings of food and to pour the drinks. Units took turns being hoppers.

Robert (Skipper) Raymond, the waterfront director, led us through the steps of learning to swim in the cold, clear water of Togue Pond. We progressed from red cap (beginner) to blue or white. He left for the Navy during the war, but he and his wife returned afterwards to lead us again.

The extremely beautiful location of Natarswi lent itself to wonderful wilderness adventures. The mountain and canoe trips were eagerly anticipated by all of us, and the majesty of Katahdin was ever-present as we swam and canoed. Most of us girls became quite proficient in handling those Old Town canoes. Climbing Katahdin, camping at Chimney Pond, crossing Knife Edge-all was always a thrill. Young as we were, the beauty of nature was not lost on us, and the sense of achievement in camping skills gave us confidence that we would put to good use in our later lives.

We girls would pile into the back of the pickup truck, sit on our sleeping bags or bed rolls, and singing all the way ride to Roaring Brook, then begin the climb to Chimney Pond, where we would roll out our bags in lean-tos. We would cook our supper over an open fire, and then gather around with the others camping up there for singing and story- telling. One memorable group had a fellow who could recite poetry; it was the first time I ever heard Robert Service's *Dangerous Dan McGrew* and *The Cremation of Sam McGee*. Besides, campers everywhere knew the same songs and could sing them for hours!

My favorite trail up the mountain was the Cathedral, across Knife Edge, and down Dudley. The trip down sliding over the huge boulders nearly always wore out the seat of my dungarees! An unforgettable sight was the early morning sunrise, or a sunset reflecting off the side of the mountain. Lights and shadows played out a beautiful scene. A stop along the trail at Diana's icy cold pool presented a challenge to see who could jump in and swim just one stroke!

The Great Northern Paper Company owned the land all around, and there were very few roads. The Golden Road had not been built then. The logs were still being sent down the rivers, so when we took canoe trips on any river we had to always watch out for logs. Natarswi girls took canoe trips on the Ambajejus, the Abol, the Jo Mary, and the West Branch of the Penobscot. On one memorable trip we watched the lumberjacks break up log jams, run the logs, and roll them. They were very good! We were invited to breakfast at their camp one morning. Although the men had long since gone into the woods to work, the cook fed us a bountiful repast. The quantity of food was amazing- oatmeal, eggs, bacon, potatoes, beans, bread and biscuits, doughnuts, pancakes, and pie! Then there was the camp coffee, the pot with the grounds in the bottom. We did the best we could!

On one side of the Ambajejus was the Boom House, with a log boom by it. A boom is a chain of logs hooked together to form a sort of fence in the water to hold logs in until they were sent down the river. The Boom House was a favorite stop of ours because we were always offered doughnuts or blueberry muffins.

We camped on the ground on canoe trips and so mosquito netting and insect repellent were necessities. We could make one-girl shelters with our ponchos, and we had to put tarps over our food supplies. We baked in reflector ovens and any of us could stir up a pot of goulash in no time! Whether or not it was really as tasty as it seemed at the time, I really don't know, but it was all consumed with great gusto!

We poled our canoes up some rapids, rode them down, and portaged around some. Wind could be a factor to be reckoned with, and it seemed as if we always forgot the "wind changer!" Skills were learned and honed until most of us were fairly proficient. I'll never forget the white birches, the dark green firs, the scent of balsam and pine, paddle blades dipping in the clear water, and always the lovely, haunting cry of the loons-the wonder of the North.

Summers spent at camp gave all of us girls a broader

insight into the lives and personalities of others. Cooperation and a sense of teamwork and responsibility created a bond among us, along with a great and abiding love of nature. Together we have a special place in our hearts for the camp and the friendships that last a lifetime.

In the summer of 1946 about 15 of us made up a Junior Guide unit. We had been preparing for this experience in previous years. We had to make trails by compass readings, set up a campsite and shelters, cook, canoe and swim, and know general information regarding our state of Maine. We were then tested by a Maine Guide. It was with great exhilaration that I received my certificate and my father presented me with my very own paddle-a treasure I still paddle with!

In 1947 and '48 we became Apprentice Counselors. I left Natarswi early in 1948 to work at Camp Roosevelt for two weeks. The Orono/Old Town Girl Scouts used this camp then, although it was a Boy Scout camp. Several girls from the Penobscot Indian Reservation attended. Two precious little girls attached themselves to me, and I felt their need for love and attention. They were quiet little girls, with deep brown eyes which took in much, but they said little. I loved these little girls and found great pleasure in working with the young children. Girl Scouting meant a great deal to me.

"The Standpipe"

The waterfront at the base of Mt. Katahdin - Camp Natarswi

Tent mates at Natarswi
Jean Welch, Lois Griffin, Jackie Beebe, Judy Wood, Jean Swetland

The old camp at Phillips Lake

Grace, Elinor, Lois at Phillips Lake
(1947)

Grace, Dad at the well - Phillips Lake

Dad at the camp - Phillips Lake

Friends: Jean, Barbara, Lois, Nancy, Sally on Hammond Street by Mishou's Drugstore

Old friends - Sally and Barbara

Lois - graduation from B.H.S. (1949)

Chapter Ten:

Final Years at Home

We left Fifth Street Junior High after three years and entered Bangor High School on Harlow Street in September of 1946. Only a few girls and boys went to private schools. My close friend, Sally, went away. However, a number of boys went off to Hebron, Ricker and the like. But students from Fifth Street and Garland Street Junior Highs came together for the three high school years. An excellent faculty led us through our studies and the school clubs. In the fall a lot of us girls played field hockey at Chapin Park, then in winter we played half court basketball at school. Saturday afternoons in fall we walked across town to Garland Street where the boys played their football games. In the winter we walked down Buck Street to the old yellow auditorium for their basketball games. If the street was really icy, sometimes we would squat down, hook our hands onto the bumper of a slow moving auto, and let it pull us along. Springtime would find us at Hayford Field cheering the baseball team on.

I belonged to the high school sorority and the Sub-Deb Club. It was all very much fun-friends, dates, wearing skirts and sweaters, and penny loafers.

Christmas of 1948 was my very last Maine Christmas; it was clear, white, cold, and wonderful, as Christmas should be. There were colored lights reflecting on snow, the wonderful smell of the balsam tree in the house, and surprises under the tree. We girls always went with our dad to select, cut, and haul a tree to the car and on to the house. He loved the holidays as much as we did, and he always had fun wrapping small things in big boxes to keep us guessing. We always had ribbon candy, and Daddy would receive at least one can of Briggs pipe tobacco, and sometimes a new pipe.

This particular Christmas, 1948, Elinor and Grace sent me a velvet and faille black dress with a sweetheart neckline. I loved it and felt quite sophisticated in it and my baby-doll pumps. We had an open house and many of my friends came. Some of us went with our Catholic friends to midnight mass. I had a steady boyfriend and we exchanged gifts. Grace had graduated from Maine in the spring of 1948 and was working in Washington, D.C. She was living with a couple of her classmates. Elinor was in North Carolina.

During the Easter break from school in the spring of 1949, Dudley and Helen took me on a trip to New York and Washington and we were gone two weeks. I was 17 years old before I had crossed the border into another state! We traveled the four-lane Merritt Parkway through Connecticut, with a stop at Yale University to see the old ivy-covered buildings on that lovely campus. We girls used to sing the Whiffenpoof Song at Natarswi, and now here I was!

Our first night was spent in Rye, New York, in a Tourist Home. From there we went to the Hotel Taft in New York City, close to the Radio City Music Hall, where we saw the Rockettes and the television filming of the opera *Aida*. We saw TV for the first time in New York that spring, shared pastries at Longe Champs, ate at the automat, and walked along 5th Avenue, where I shopped for a pale green sun dress. Much to my amazement, people danced in the afternoon at the Taft! Guy Lombardo played live music and I danced there with my father.

From there we went to Washington, D.C. My parents stayed in a tourist home, the forerunner of the Bed and Breakfast, and I stayed in the apartment with Grace, Martha, and Syd. It was great fun. The girls took me to Hogates where daiquiris were ordered and the band played various state songs for their customers. When the "Maine Stein Song" was played, all Mainers in the restaurant stood up and sang along!

We were invited to the home of an old friend of Dad's with whom he had worked in World War I. He was a delightful gentleman, and we were served a southern dinner by waiters in his gracious Maryland home. It was my first dinner of real fried chicken and spoon bread. Delicious! Then Senator Brewster of Maine granted us passes to attend a session of the Senate and we ate in the Senate Dining Hall. The cherry blossoms were beautiful as we toured buildings, monuments, and museums. We spent a day at Mt. Vernon. It was a wonderful, enriching trip.

Back home in Bangor, ice was leaving the lakes and

streams, snow was melting away, and spring green was reappearing. Mud finally dries up, apple blossoms and lilacs appear and spring cleaning is carried out. I wrote my senior essay. There was a total lack of guidance for future school endeavors, and I had no idea of what I really wanted to do. I did not know when I put on the white gown and cap with the maroon tassel and marched across the stage in the old yellow Bangor auditorium to receive my diploma, that in a few months I would be at Peabody College in Nashville, Tennessee.

We live on in the lives of those we touch, and they live on in us. We can go home again in our hearts and minds, the home that molded and shaped us. My home was Bangor.

Printed in the United States
25387LVS00001B/215-238

9 780976 494003